Bye-Bye, Bully!

A Kid's Guide for Dealing With Bullies

Written by
J. S. Jackson

Illustrated by
R. W. Alley

ONE
CARING
PLACE

Abbey Press
St. Meinrad, IN 47577

This is for my four terrific boys—Steve, John, Joey, and Danny—who have all been exposed to bullying in their lives, and have come through it strong, healthy, and happy. And also for my wonderful wife, Molly Wigand, without whose talent, inspiration, and support, I could barely lift a finger.

First hardcover edition 2010

Text © 2003 J. S. Jackson
Illustrations © 2003 St. Meinrad Archabbey
Published by One Caring Place
Abbey Press
St. Meinrad, Indiana 47577

Library of Congress Catalog Number
2002111571

ISBN 978-0-87029-442-6

Printed in the United States of America

A Message to Parents, Teachers, and Other Caring Adults

Bullying—the repeated malicious torment of a child—has become a pervasive form of harassment in many elementary schools. In some studies, over 75 percent of all students say they have been the target of bullying.

Bullying is always about an "imbalance of power": physical, emotional, or social. Generally, boys tend to employ physical power (pushing, hitting, arm-twisting), while girls hurt others through social power (teasing, gossiping, or rumor-spreading).

Until recently, bullying has often been considered a "kids will be kids" problem. Teasing, in particular, is often taken lightly, considered to be a way of "toughening up" children, making them ready for the real world.

In reality, bullying takes a serious toll on children. People who were bullied as children are more likely to suffer from depression and low self-esteem in later life. Conversely, those who were the bullies in childhood often carry that behavior with them into adulthood and are more likely to engage in criminal activity.

The best way to safeguard children from becoming victims of bullies is to teach them how to be assertive. This involves encouraging children to express their feelings clearly, to say "no" when they feel pressured or uncomfortable, to stand up for themselves verbally without fighting, and to walk away from more dangerous situations. Bullies are less likely to intimidate children who are confident and resourceful.

Also, encourage children to share information about school and school-related activities. Pay attention to the following symptoms that may indicate a child is being bullied: withdrawal, abrupt lack of interest in school, a drop in grades, or signs of physical abuse. If these danger signs are present, contact the child's teacher and develop a plan of action.

Children cannot handle bullying alone. By modeling compassionate behavior and equipping children with the coping tools they need, parents and educators can help prevent and reverse this cruel epidemic.

—*J. S. Jackson*

What Is Bullying?

If someone teases you, hurts you, or is just plain mean to you—day after day, week after week—that is called "bullying."

Bullying is different from the little bumps, pushes, or arguments kids sometimes get into. Bullying is not an accident. It is hurting another person, on purpose, over and over again.

Is there someone on your school bus or the playground who is often just mean to other kids—punching, hitting, or kicking them? Is there someone in your classroom who is always making fun of another kid? That is how bullies act.

You Are Not Alone

Almost everybody is bullied at some time in his life...by a brother or sister, a neighborhood kid, or a classmate.

If someone bullies you, it can make you feel scared, helpless, and alone. But there are things kids can do to stop bullying.

Remember: No one deserves to be bullied. By learning more about bullying, you will be better able to handle this problem if it happens to you.

What Do Bullies Look Like?

Bullies come in all shapes and sizes. You can tell bullies more by how they act than by how they look.

Bullies are often loud, selfish, and pushy. They need to do things and get things that make them feel powerful. They will use and hurt other people to get what they want.

Kids who are bullies try to make *themselves* feel good by making *others* feel bad. The funny thing is, they do this because, deep down, they feel bad themselves. If they can push around other kids, it makes them feel more powerful.

Who Do Bullies Bother?

Bullies look for people they think are weaker or scared of them. They often pick on people who are small, shy, or different.

Are you "different" in any way? Do you wear glasses? Do you have red hair? Are you kind of thin or chubby? Are you tall or short for your age? Do you speak with an accent?

God gave you a special look and personality to make you the great, one-of-a-kind person you are! "Different" doesn't mean *better* or *worse*—it just means *different*. Be proud and happy—you are exactly the way God meant you to be!

How Bullies Hurt Others

A bully might corner a kid in the back of the school bus and punch him or twist his arm. Or push someone down on the playground. Or pull a girl's hair in the bathroom.

Bullies also hurt kids' feelings, by teasing or calling them names. A bully might call a boy with large ears "Dumbo," or a girl with red hair "Carrot Top." This kind of teasing can be just as hurtful as the hitting kind.

Sometimes a bully might whisper about you, laugh at you, and make you feel as if no one likes you. It hurts your feelings to be left out, not part of any group.

What Bullies Want

Bullies like the feeling of power they get from making other people feel bad. Here are some examples of what bullies do, and what they want *you* to do. If you want to stop a bully, try not to act the way the bully wants you to!

What a Bully Does	What a Bully Wants You to Do
hit, push, or knock you down	cry, run away
call you names: "Hey, Four Eyes!" "Hi there, Fatty!"	cry, feel sad and ashamed
talk behind your back	cry, feel bad and alone

Four Ways to Stop Bullies

Because not all kids are the same, and not all bullies are the same, you need to try different ways to stop them. Four of the best ways to stop bullies are:

1. Stand up for yourself. Act strong.
2. Steer clear of trouble.
3. Put a "safety cloud" around yourself.
4. Tell a grown-up. Ask for help.

Stand Up for Yourself

Bullies don't pick on kids who stand up for themselves. Practice this in front of a mirror:

- Stand up tall and proud.
- Look yourself straight in the eye.
- Say out loud: "I don't like what you're doing and I want you to stop it."
- Say this over and over until you sound like you really mean it.

The next time a bully starts picking on you, you'll be ready. Stand up tall. Look him in the eye, and say, "I don't like what you're doing and I want you to stop it." Keep on saying it till he stops.

Stay Out of the Way of Trouble

Steer clear of bullies and they won't be able to hurt you.

If a bully bothered you in the back of the school bus yesterday, make sure to sit in the front today. If someone keeps trying to trip you on the playground, try to find a friend or two to keep around you, or stay near the teacher in charge. If someone teases you, just say, "Whatever..." and keep walking.

There's a big difference between being a "chicken" and being plain smart. Staying out of the way of trouble, when you can, is smart.

Put a "Cloud" Around Yourself

Here's a great way to deal with any kind of teasing or name-calling. Ask God to put a "Safety Cloud" or "Power Cloud" around you to protect you.

Pretend that you are inside a beautiful, warm, happy cloud that God has created just for you. While you are in this cloud, you can't really see the bully or hear what she's saying. You are safe and fine, wrapped in God's love.

Putting a cloud around yourself stops bullying, because the bully does not get what she wants. She is not able to bother you.

"Telling" Is Not "Tattling"

If nothing else works, it's time to tell an adult what's going on and ask for help. Sometimes it's hard for kids to ask for help, especially if they've been told not to "tattle." But there's a big difference between *tattling* and *telling*.

You might tattle on your sister for dumping out a whole box of crayons on the floor. Tattling is usually done just to get someone else in trouble. And it's usually about something that's not very hurtful.

But when a bully is hurting someone, you need to tell a grown-up. In this case, you are trying to get someone out of trouble—the person being hurt. Telling an adult is the right thing to do!

Are You Ever a Bully?

All of us are mean to others at times—when we're tired, or mad, or just in a bad mood.

If you are feeling mean, try to remember how much it hurts when someone is mean to you. Try to deal with bad feelings in a good way—maybe by going out and hitting tennis balls really hard, or by talking out your feelings with someone.

Take the "Pledge to Stop Bullying":

1. I will not bully other students, friends, neighbors, or family members.
2. I will help others who are being bullied.
3. I will try to be kind to all kids all the time.

Helping Others Handle Bullies

If you see a bully picking on someone, you might be afraid to do anything. Try to find your courage, and say, "Stop it!" or "That's enough!" or "Quit doing that!" You will be amazed at what happens, especially if other kids start speaking up too.

If you see someone being teased, you can use another kind of courage. Go up to the person being teased, treat her like a friend, and ask if she wants to do something with you.

A little courage goes a long way in stopping bullies!

No More Bullying

Kids have the power to stop bullies. Find your courage and stick up for yourself and others.

The holy writings of many faiths give us this "Golden Rule": "Treat others the way you would like to be treated." If everyone obeyed this rule, there would be no more bullying.

You can help make your home, school, and neighborhood "bully-free zones." Every person has the right to feel safe and happy. Together, kids, parents, and teachers can make it happen.

J. S. Jackson is a husband, dad, and writer living in Lenexa, Kansas. The former manager of Hallmark Cards' creative writing staff, he is now a freelance writer/editor for Abbey Press. A multi-tasking "Mr. Mom," he creates cards, books, and other inspirational materials from his messy home office. He is presently in the process of writing a book called *Safe at Home*, about how important it is for kids to feel safe in their home environment.

R. W. Alley is the illustrator for the popular Abbey Press adult and children's series of Elf-help books, as well as an illustrator and writer of other children's books. He lives in Barrington, Rhode Island, with his wife, daughter, and son. See a wide variety of his works at: www.rwalley.com.